Walks on and Woodbury C

Chips Barber

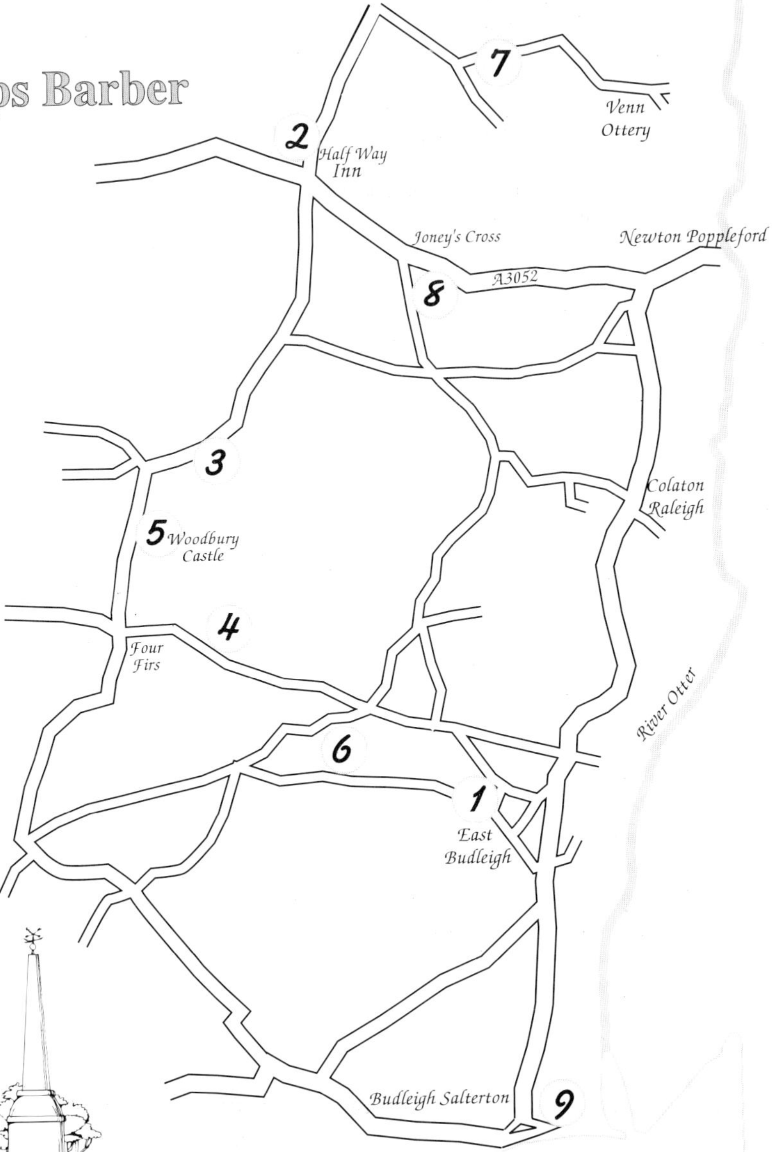

OBELISK PUBLICATIONS

Other 'Walking' titles ...

Diary of a Dartmoor Walker, Chips Barber
Diary of a Devonshire Walker, Chips Barber
The Great Walks of Dartmoor, Terry Bound
Ten Family Walks on Dartmoor, Sally and Chips Barber
Ten Family Walks in East Devon, Sally and Chips Barber
Walks in the Shadow of Dartmoor, Denis McCallum
Walks in Tamar and Tavy Country, Denis McCallum
Six Short Pub Walks on Dartmoor, Sally and Chips Barber
The Templer Way, Derek Beavis
Walks in the Chagford Countryside, Terry Bound
Walks in the Totnes Countryside, Bob Mann
Walks in the South Hams, Brian Carter
Pub Walks in the South Hams, Brian Carter
Pub Walks in and around The Haldon Hill, Brian Carter
Nine Short Pub Walks in and around Torbay, Brian Carter
Circular Walks on Eastern Dartmoor, Liz Jones

We have over 150 Devon titles. For a full list of current books, please contact us at Obelisk Publications, 2 Church Hill, Pinhoe, Exeter, Devon, EX4 9ER or telephone (01392) 468556.

Acknowledgements

Many thanks to Rodney Helme and Steve Othen for their help.
All photos by or belonging to Chips Barber
except page 15 from the collection of George Pridmore.
All sketch maps redrawn from an out-of-copyright source by Sally Barber.

First published in 1998 by
Obelisk Publications, 2 Church Hill, Pinhoe, Exeter, Devon
Designed by Chips and Sally Barber
Typeset by Sally Barber
Printed in Great Britain by
Greenhill Press

Walks on and around Woodbury Common

Woodbury Common is, for some, the Dartmoor of East Devon. An area of rolling moorlands, complete with its own authentic valley bogs, it certainly does resemble, in part, a small scale version of its illustrious larger western counterpart. However, Woodbury Common has a much lower elevation and only rises to about 600 feet above sea level, a fact which means that it experiences far less rainfall – about half as much – than Dartmoor (but please don't quote me if it pours with rain when you go for a walk there!). It is an important venue for leisure and recreation, the area being used for all sorts of energetic activities like mountain biking, golf, orienteering, horse riding, jogging and, of course, courting!

The Royal Marines have used the common for many years for their training and it is not unusual for 'ordinary' bushes to suddenly turn into camouflaged figures, so a wary eye is recommended! Traces of the Marines' historic connections with the common are liberally scattered around, and will be seen on some of these short circular outings, as well as the current-day obstacles designed for training sessions, for example the water tunnels and 'Smartie tubes' which have featured on many television documentaries. Today, 'live' ammunition is restricted to the grenade range and the entire area has, officially, been cleared but lethal artifacts from the Second World War may still surface from time to time, so it is imperative that if you discover 'metal objects' – don't pick them up!

Although it is the norm to refer to this area as Woodbury Common it should be made clear that really it is a series of commons which, in the main, draw their names from settlements at their base.

So we find these East Devon 'Commons' – Aylesbeare, Venn Ottery, Harpford, Colaton Raleigh, Withycombe Raleigh, Woodbury, Bicton, East Budleigh, Lympstone, Shortwood and Dalditch – all more or less joined together and all part of the same geological formation. At their widest point they are about a mile wide but in a general north–south direction they run for about seven

miles, culminating in the high cliffs called 'The Floors' between Budleigh Salterton and Sandy Bay. Characteristic are the rounded stones on the top of the pebblebed heaths, which are locally known as 'popples' – as in Newton Poppleford! Their roundness is the result of water action, the top of the commons once being the bed of an enormous river that flowed from France, long before the formation of the English Channel.

On a fine day the many car parks are well patronised as it has become a time-honoured tradition for people 'to go up on the common for an hour or two'. The most favoured activity seems to be sitting in the car in the stony car park opposite Woodbury Castle, on the edge of the common's steep scarp slope. From this vantage point, on a clear day, a considerable area can be seen: the Exe Estuary; the Haldon Hills beyond; Exeter to the right of this; the coastline from Dawlish Warren around to Berry Head, to the left; and in the background on the far horizons, Dartmoor, the roof of Devon. A lot of folk add to the Woodbury passive experience by having an ice-cream and/or a snooze! However, by acquiring this book you have shown a willingness to explore this lovely part of the county. I hope you will not get lost on these walks because, despite its small size, it is easy to misread or misinterpret directions when there are so many possible paths to follow. The maze of tracks that crisscross the common go in all directions and there are many paths which exist in reality but are not portrayed on the map. The same applies to much of the woodland. For those who like to follow them when out for a stroll they can be quite baffling, and it is not unknown for those who get hopelessly lost to claim that they have been pixy-led!

The maps of the district only seem to record long-established tracks so don't rely too much on them for your exact whereabouts.

It is a sad reflection of life that I have to tell you to remove any valuables from your car as there are always those of a mind to steal. Remember to lock all doors and … beware of cowboys as well!

1 – Around and About East Budleigh

There is a car park just below the church in East Budleigh where you are welcome to park free of charge for up to 23 hours. This should be long enough for even the slowest stroller as this walk is just under two miles. There are modern toilets on one side of the car park entrance and a stone bearing an information board on the opposite side.

This, if you are keen to know more about the history of the area, tells you about the village and some of the nearby landmarks. The 'East' in the parish and the hundred's name wasn't added until the fifteenth century and until then it was simply known as 'Budley' as shown on Bicton Cross (1743).

Turn left out of the car park into Hayes Lane and walk straight ahead to the T-junction where the pub, formerly the King's Arms but now the Sir Walter Raleigh, and the lane's name sign now reflect the local ties of one of the great characters of English history – but will he appear in ghostly form to lay down his cloak for us when we meet the inevitable damp spots along the lanes?

Turn right into the High Street to cross the small bridge over the Budleigh Brook. The view back over your shoulder has been the standard picture postcard view of the village ever since photography began although street furniture and vehicles make it harder to capture a rural scene than in times past.

Pass the imposing Wynard's on your right, and the village hall on your left. Continue along the right side of the road until Drake's School is reached. Turn right, on the bending road, into a lane at Wynard's Farm where a sign refers to the Cottles herd. It's always inspiring to see the sign 'Unsuitable for Motors' and there is one here which, apart from agricultural vehicles, almost assures walkers and horse riders that they won't be too troubled by traffic.

This gently rising pedestrian thoroughfare is Hayeswood Lane, but the fields sloping down to it on either side are steep. Soon a track, Little Down Lane, leads off to the left and another, Lillage Lane, a short way ahead, tails off to the right but both of these should be ignored in favour of the way straight ahead past the matching pair of road signs. Green is the predominant colour in the landscape ahead, the valley reducing views to the immediate fields and woods.

Hayeswood Lane eventually starts to steepen and the track is decidedly sunken as it climbs the hillside. Ferns occupy the claustrophobic, often muddy, twilight corridor but all is not doom and gloom, for the path levels out, the oppressive hedges reduce in height and a double gateway, complete with footpaths signed away from us on both sides, is reached at the top of the rise.

The gateway to our right is the one which most concerns us. The view beyond the stile looks across to Peak Hill above Sidmouth and the triangular shaped hill to its right is High Peak.

Cross this stile and, using the sleepers, avoid the muddy gateway's primeval ooze. The path is very obvious and follows the left-hand hedge. Soon almost all of East Budleigh village is in sight. After a dip another stile is reached and once more you are treated to the tricky task of negotiating it.

The first yards across the field ahead are parallel with the telegraph posts, but the path swings under them to drop downhill to another stile. The view up the Otter Valley is a fine one.

A cart track takes us onwards to our next and final stile today but as our technique has been honed to perfection, the leaping of it into the lane beyond is just a formality.

Turn left here, and soon heading downhill along Lillage Lane will bring you to the surfaced Hayes Lane, the one which goes up to Hayes Barton, Raleigh's birthplace. On the junction is an electricity sub-station giving out a constant humming sound. Although it bears some semblance to a modern work of art, its 'beauty' is questioned by the placement of conifers around it to help stop it being a 33,000-volt blot on the landscape.

Turn right here and mosey along this quiet lane back to East Budleigh. Soon the speed reduction signs are met, and just beyond them on the right is the thatched and haunted Vicarsmead. What a history this ancient house, dating back to 1485, has; and although it appears to be in the heart of the countryside it had a reputation as being the headquarters of an eighteenth century smuggling organisation. The house is honeycombed with passages and there are many 'hidey-holes' where contraband could have been stowed away and probably was! The clergy were heavily involved in this illicit trade and none more so than the Rev Ambrose Stapleton, vicar of East Budleigh from 1794 to 1852, when his Maker decided to 'smuggle him' up to Heaven. In between, the good vicar preached and smuggled. He was reputed to have such a loud voice that he could be heard from the small bridge just beyond Vicarsmead – 300 yards from his church! Ambrose was also an eminently practical man for when it rained during a burial, he conducted the service from the relative comfort of a sentry box. When this eventually fell apart he moved to the shelter of the vestry window, almost a funeral by remote control!

Matthew Munday was another parson to live at Vicarsmead to be heavily involved in the illegal importation of brandy and tobacco. Another later resident of this house was Susannah Gibbons who, when she wasn't as a nimble as she used to be, had a special wheeled cart made. This was harnessed to a donkey and regularly used for her journeys to the church. Her daughter, Maria, years later, used the same cart, plus a bonus donkey for extra pulling power, to explore Devon. The product of these adventures was a number of books which give an insight into what life in Devon was like in a bygone age. The best-known was *We Donkeys in Devon*. Mother and daughter are both buried in the church on the slope ahead of us, as are the many husbands of a lady Maria wrote about. She tells how James Lackington, a well-known London bookseller, from Budleigh Salterton, passed away on 15 November 1815 having used up his quota of three score years and ten. His widow didn't mourn too long because she married three men in quick succession, all of them passing away and being buried in the graveyard at East Budleigh's church. Miss Gibbons wrote, "Surely few women have been married three times in one church and have laid four husbands in the yard that surrounds it." Although unfortunately phrased, she went on to add that the merry widow married one more time but that the fifth lucky chap was buried at Exeter.

In the past East Budleigh's bellringers, on hearing rumbles of thunder, would hasten to the church. Here they would quickly give the bells a ring and in next to no time the thunderstorm would be dispersed from the district, so it's said.

We now pass over a small road bridge over the ever-babbling, never running dry, Budleigh Brook by Hill Farm, noted for its 'Budleigh Herd of Golden Guernseys', to head the short distance back to the car park and the end of this pleasant little stroll. The Budleigh Brook used to drive at least three mills between the common and the Otter, these being Hayes Mill, Higher Budleigh manor mill and Thorn Mill, downstream and close to its junction with the Otter. The church, All Saints, if open, is worth a visit and makes a good history lesson, the bench ends being of particular interest in local history circles.

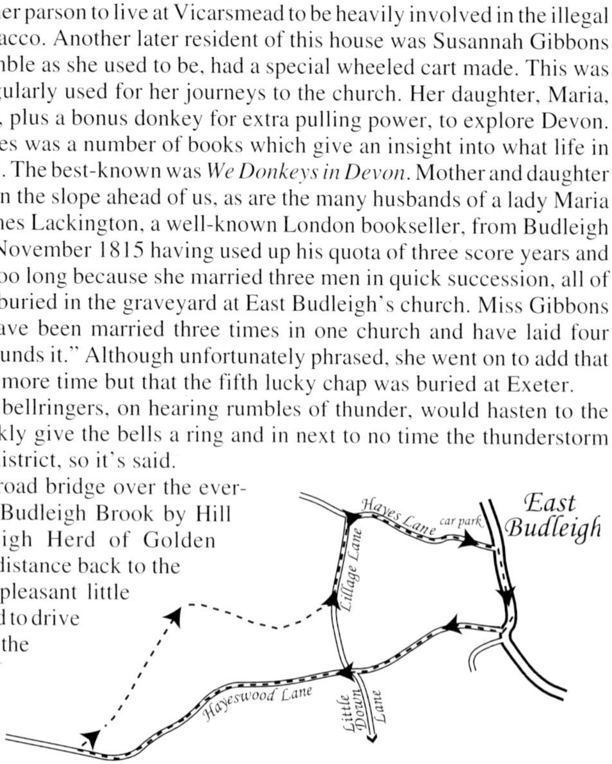

2 – On the Trail of the Lonesome Pine

The place for parking for this walk of about two miles, where there's room for a small number of cars, is about 100 yards along the road towards Ottery St Mary from the Half Way Inn. This is beside the turning to Aylesbeare.

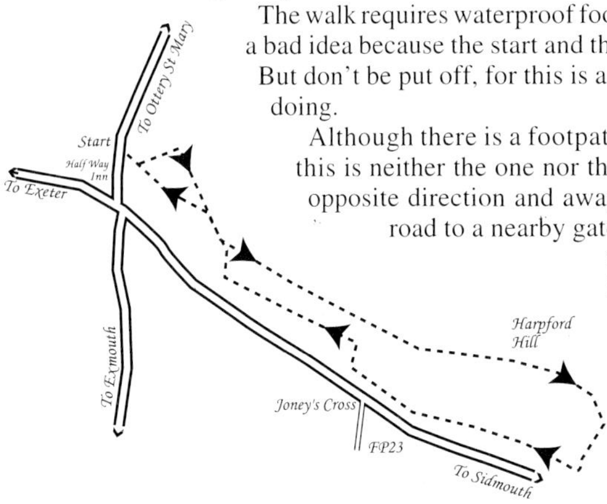

The walk requires waterproof footwear, so wellington boots would not be a bad idea because the start and the end are likely to be extremely muddy. But don't be put off, for this is a pleasant stroll and one which I enjoyed doing.

Although there is a footpath leading off beside this parking place this is neither the one nor the direction to go. Carefully walk in the opposite direction and away from the Half Way Inn and cross the road to a nearby gateway with a stile. Cross it and follow in the wake of the various horse riders who have helped make this thoroughfare that bit softer underfoot, or hoof. The going is soft to squelchy and the vegetation becomes more intrusive. After about 100 yards or so there is a forking in the ways so, although it's not a clear path, veer left onto a curving, twisting way between trees. Stay with it until a small stream is reached emerging from the field beyond. Although you won't be drowned, do be aware of the miry ground beside it. Having crossed it a fork is reached; take the right branch. This leads to the open common and a more open aspect as the narrow track drops downhill to a series of newly created ponds. Pass between them to reach a broad path making a T-junction. Turn right and follow it around and up the hillside ignoring all alternative side paths. Embedded in the ground are symbols of this part of the county, the rounded bunter pebbles, many of them orange in colour and some quite large. If you haven't noticed yet, these rounded stones have been used in buildings and walls in the villages below the commons and make even the most ordinary wall an ornate feature.

To your left and ahead is Aylesbeare Common which, despite its quiet appearance today, has seen plenty of action. In 1804 troops from the Wiltshire Militia and the Bedfordshire Militia were billeted here, this being their temporary HQ for the duration of their stay.

In the First World War there was a Portuguese timber camp on Aylesbeare Common. These prisoners of war spoke little English so Anibel de Conchicho Alves, who was Portuguese but not a prisoner of war, volunteered to be their interpreter. Apparently, almost every time that he needed to converse with the English authorities it was to complain about something. The dialogue usually centred on the numerous hutments on the common, these not being up to the standards that the POWs expected, or the fact that the men were, all too often, cold and hungry. With such great loss of life in the trenches in France and Belgium there was little sympathy for the plight of the Portuguese. Alas, poor Anibel got himself into some strife as the English authorities believed that he was the cause of the unrest. He was summoned to HQ in London and was escorted to the railway station. However, he refused to board the train and was thus charged for his indiscipline thereby ending up behind bars in an English gaol and therefore in a far worse predicament than his fellow countrymen on Aylesbeare Common!

It's been suggested that American troops were also here preparing for the D-Day landings and that gear, surplus to their requirements, was buried on Aylesbeare Common, but talk like this is repeated all around the country and it's unlikely that you will be staring down the barrel of a Sherman tank if you disturb the surface.

Towards the brow of the hill two broader tracks lead off right and left, both marked with green painted posts. Ignore the invitation and continue onwards where the going levels out. To your right is the hilltop feature of a tall, thin, but somewhat bereft-of-life tree, our 'Lonesome Pine'. For the time being we pass well to the left of it to reach a surfaced road. The track we want lies just a few yards to the left of this T-junction and continues the trend in the direction of travel that we are following. Now it's gentle downhill stuff, staying with the broadest path, with views over the Otter valley as the path, easy to walk, wends its way across the heath. Some way down the hillside it veers sharply to the right to head towards the Exeter-Sidmouth road, which now lies straight ahead and just beyond the trees. As you reach the gap in the trees you will see a path going left down the hill and another just beyond turning right up the slope. Both are marked with posts tipped in green paint and the latter is the one we take. For the next few hundred yards this path runs parallel to the main road, the green posts guiding you back up over the common. Although you will hear the traffic you won't be subjected to the fumes. The path passes between almost impenetrable, head-high vegetation, almost like a maze and gets ever closer to the main road without actually getting to it. Aylesbeare Common is an important nature reserve with a vast number of creatures living here, hopefully in peace and undisturbed by the hand of Man.

'The Lonesome Pine' is now seen again, straight ahead, as the path reaches the surfaced, private road to Woolcombes. Don't turn left towards the main road and Joney's Cross but go through the gateway. Here there is a sign for the East Devon Way, a long-distance inland path of 40 miles between the rivers Exe and Lym, created in the 1990s.

Take the path up to the hilltop tree and you will pass right beside our 'Lonesome Pine'. Just beyond, along this green path, on the left, is a trig point. Stay with the path which, after a hundred yards or so, veers left and then right to head towards woodland. This it only skirts to start its fall from higher ground. To the left of the path is a wide bench, placed there to the memory of Frank Michael Wright (1957–1992) and established by his parents.

In a few hundred yards we meet the track that we climbed earlier. This time we turn left, ignoring any further green posts, and continue down the hillside until we reach a fork marked by a yellow arrow. Beyond the trees the Half Way Inn can be just spied. Bear left here and continue down to 'enjoy' the wettest part of the walk occurring just when you thought it was safe. This is an exceedingly wet area, the stream at the bottom of the dip is probably the driest, and the cleanest, part of this section, where the deliciously soft and oozy bog runs up the slope beyond. Persevere with the path, which will take you back along the narrow lane where the walk started earlier.

It's known that once upon a time horse races were held nearby on a regular basis. 'Aylesbeare Races' were run, during the late 1870s and early 1880s, in the fields below this popular wayside inn on the west-facing slopes of the hill. By all accounts it was something of a ramshackle event for it was not uncommon for the one o'clock race to go off at three! The course was about half a mile in extent, the land being lent, for the event, by Mr Edward Johnson of Farringdon House. A rule was established that any race had to have a minimum of three runners. The winners often had to wait up to a week to be presented with their prizes for being first past the post, these rewards being presented at the Half Way Inn, which now awaits you should you have a thirst or an appetite – preferably after a change of footwear!

3 – Across and Under Colaton Raleigh Common

This walk starts from the 'Tumulus' car park on the B3180 about a quarter of a mile to the north-east of Woodbury Castle. A tumulus is an ancient burial mound and there are several tumuli in this area. This small one, like many others, has trees growing from it. Park your vehicle here, remembering as usual, to secrete any valuables out of sight or, if they are portable, take them on this pleasant walk which is just under three miles. Part of the route is along the edge of the Colaton Raleigh Common grenade range and if red flags or lamps are displayed then firing is in progress. Advance warning notices are printed in the local press but if you have missed them and prefer to try one of the other walks, none are too far away to be too much of an inconvenience. But should you decide to go ahead on this walk, sentries will direct you, in a pleasant manner, around the 'Danger Area' and the detour will not add much to the length of the walk. It is worth noting that no firing ever takes place on a Sunday.

At the farthest end of the car park from the road a distinct track leads off in a southerly direction. Follow it for about 60 yards, to the left of an isolated tree, until it meets a four-crossway of paths. If it's a fine day then you might notice the shining sea near Budleigh Salterton. Peak Hill above Sidmouth is another distinct feature.

Turn left and follow the track. If you know this landscape you will be able to see to your right, in the distance, the small cliff bluff at the mouth of the Otter and the line of pine trees that runs up to it. After about 400 yards you will reach another clump of trees where many tracks converge. Your way onwards is straight across and beyond it, a blue arrow giving you a pointer as to the right way to go. Just yards beyond this junction you are offered a further choice of ways but take the left fork and maintain the level. Walking beside the track is drier than on it where puddles have accumulated in some of the more non-porous ruts. It's quite likely that this track is an old coaching route, because it follows the alignment of a former route which ran from a point close to Woodbury Castle down the north-eastern flank of the common to Hawkerland, the exact same direction that we are now travelling. This was the roughest part of a route that rose from the Exe Estuary and headed on beyond the common to Newton Poppleford, in the Otter valley, where it passed the old toll house in the village (this being the oldest one in Devon, dating back to 1758), before heading ever eastwards along the south coast of England. By the time the passengers had crossed Woodbury Common they would have been quite shaken up. At Newton Poppleford they could wait at the toll house and pick up the London-bound coach.

For us, though, it's Shanks' pony but the going is easy and soon starts to drop from the ridge. To the left is the Hawkerland Valley and beyond that 'The Lonesome Pine' visited on the previous stroll. In the distance ahead can be seen the unusual Dumpdon Hill, near Honiton, a most distinct Otter valley landmark. Stay with the blue arrows continuing downhill. Soon trees come right up to our track, which is joined by another path from the left. Continue onwards and downwards 'on the main drag'. Eventually the track reaches a damp dip to rise slightly, to Fire Point 19, before again dropping more sharply downhill still with the main trackway. A padlocked log, one of many designed to keep vehicles off the open common, is reached but I firmly advise even the most lithe walkers not to limbo dance under it! Continue downhill for about another fifty yards and then turn sharp right, initially almost doubling back, onto a path signposted by the fainter blue arrow. The track for the next half mile or so is much narrower. For the most part it follows the boundary between the open common, on your immediate right and farmland, on your immediate left. The land use either side of it could hardly contrast any more and it's all down to the geology.

In gaps through the trees it's just possible to spot on a nearby wooded hillside a feature that many might not notice. On a low hill just to the east is a plantation called Baker's Brake. Within this wood, and on private land where there is no public access, is a tower which protrudes just above the treetops. It was built in those days long before planning permission was necessary – when first constructed it was a more distinct landmark. It was created at the behest of Lady Rolle, in about 1840, as a most unusual birthday present for her husband. He had been ill and this would have, no doubt, cheered him up. The spiral staircase of 120 steps was designed to be wide enough to accommodate a special chair which was carried up by two attentive footmen. There were three storeys and the rooms in it were comfortably furnished. Some time later Lady Rolle used the building to store a vast collection of china, assembled from all over the world, and the structure was then referred to as 'The China Tower'. Alas, times change and during the Second World War troops did not treat the tower itself like a piece of precious porcelain and the building took something of a battering.

Stay with the path, which for the most part is level, easy walking, until a track comes down the hillside from your right to reach a gate into a field. Having noticed a few orange bricks embedded in the ground, cross over this track and resume the trek along the base of the open common. Soon a small stream is crossed with little difficulty. Its valley on the common is quite a deep one, and those troops who have trained on exercises which take them across similar ones will tell you that most of them have valley bogs like the ones found on Dartmoor. These can be very wet, 'stuggy' affairs and are well worth avoiding.

Beyond the stream the track begins to rise but stay with it.

Soon a public bridleway is reached. Don't turn left down the lane but turn right uphill and along this path. After 70 yards another blue arrow pointing left gives you the way to go. Almost before you know it another stream percolating its way down from the open common is reached. This time the benevolent hand of Man

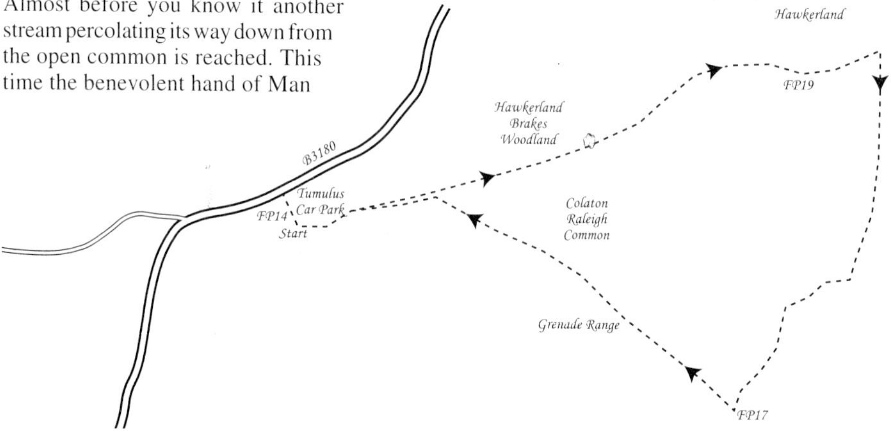

has been instrumental in the placement of timber sleepers to enable walkers to pass over this watery obstacle with minimum discomfort. The track rollercoasters for a short way, taking a slightly higher route to avoid a gully. In a few hundred yards, or so, a broad track coming down the hillside is met. Now it's time to bid farewell to the blue-arrowed way which has led us thus far. Here we turn right to ascend the steeper slopes of Colaton Raleigh Common. Soon this becomes an even broader thoroughfare as it passes 'Fire Point 17' to reach a barbed-wire, fenced-off area reserved for grenade throwing practice. It is this part of the common where red flags or lamps would prohibit access if the military were in action.

It's common knowledge, to those who regularly walk Dartmoor, when walking on firing ranges, past and present, that metal objects should not be picked up. Over the years there have been some terrible accidents on Dartmoor but, similarly, there have also been problems on Woodbury Common. In December 1952 a tragic incident took place near here, resulting in the death of a 15-year-old lad. David Lee had cycled, with three friends from Exeter, up to the common. He picked up an object on the Royal Marine mortar range, completely unaware that it might be 'live', and tossed it playfully in the direction of some of his friends. The ensuing blast killed him.

The broad path skirts the enclosed area to reach a flag pole where two tracks fork. Take the left fork. If you have a good sense of direction you will have spotted the clump of trees where we parked earlier but to get back to it needs a bit more effort.

At the next fork, just 40 yards farther on, bear right. Eventually the track reaches the other clump of trees that we passed earlier. Turn left here and follow the track to the next crossways where you will see that the obvious way to go is right, to regain your vehicle.

4 – A Circumnavigation of Woodbury Castle

The car park at 'Uphams' by the road between Four Firs Cross and Yettington is the starting place for this four-miles-long 'adventure', and some of it is really challenging to those accustomed to easier paths, on and around Woodbury Common. If you are approaching from Four Firs you will pass a number of car parks on your left, and Uphams (Fire Point 11) is just over half a mile down the road from the crossroads. These 'Fire Points' are found all over the commons. Their numbers enable fire crews to locate more precisely heathland blazes. The numbers coincide with the Royal Marines' own numeration system but their numbers are preceded with the letters RV for 'rendezvous'.

Walk out of the car park entrance and go straight across the road onto a narrow track. This is soon met by a broader one but ignore it in favour of the downward path straight ahead. The track drops down the hillside skirting the left edge of the butts of a rifle range used throughout the Second World War and abandoned in 1946. The dip below is extremely boggy but the good news is that you shouldn't get too wet, as you can easily cross the first stream to make the fairly firm straight track beyond it, which is fringed by boggy ground. In a short time, and just down the slope, another small stream is encountered at the base of a steeper slope. It doesn't provide much of an obstacle so cross it and ascend the slope, which has some steps to make the climb easier. At the top of the steps, and in the trees, there are more remains connected with this former 'danger area'. Again the path sidesteps left to skirt the wood and pass over a small rise.

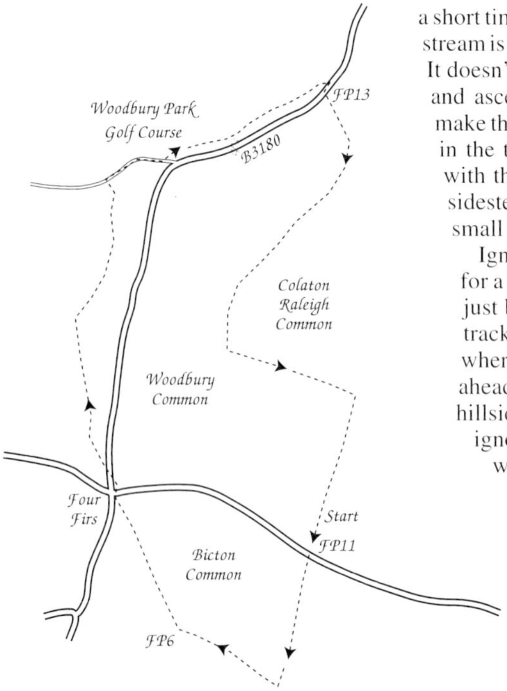

Ignoring other paths off, stay with this path for a little longer until it makes a 'T-junction', just beyond these trees, with a much broader track. Turn right here and head up the hillside, where you will see about a quarter of a mile ahead of you a distinct clump of trees on the hillside. However, to reach this you will need to ignore other possible tracks and paths, some with Royal Marine training tunnels on them.

Beyond the brow you will observe that to reach this clump you will first have to descend into another little valley complete with mandatory watery obstacle. There's always a catch! This is part of the famous endurance course featured in many television documentaries, including *Blue Peter*, and used by charitable organisations for gruelling fund-raising events. This one won't delay you as a plank is provided for a safe dry passage before the steep 'S-shaped' track is followed up the hill to those trees, which we seem to have made a big deal out of, but when we get up to them we hardly give a second look. The track skirts their right hand side to reach a brow and a crossroads. To your left is the immense quarry of Black Hill, a misnomer if ever there was one, for there is a distinct orange glow to the quarried products here. Although this area doesn't seem too spooky it has had its moments...

The details are sketchy but the message is clear. When you do this walk don't look out for the ghostly white horse that has been seen here many times! Doom and gloom will surely follow, so it's said, if you see this spectral steed, so it's best to reverse the roles and walk blinkered yourselves! This crossroads of tracks, with the quarry to your left, and a small plantation to the right, in front of you, marks another change of direction. From here turn right and walk along the broad path, keeping the trees to your left, until you reach the corner of the coniferous wood in a short distance. Do not turn the corner to skirt the wood but examine the fork of tracks ahead. Take the left one which will see you reach, with good ground conditions, the car park at Four Firs Cross. Leave the car park's exit close to the junction of roads. Immediately opposite are a number of possible paths, as is the norm for these East Devon commons. Ignore the first to the right and at the next fork, just yards away, bear left. This little path cuts the corner between the road down from Woodbury Castle and the one to Yettington. Following it for a short distance takes you to cross the road, which you will do with the utmost of care, onto a 'Public Bridleway' which is to be the route for the better part of the next mile. Initially it affords good views over parts of the Exe Estuary and also beyond to the Haldon Hills and distant Dartmoor. But soon it drops down the hillside whilst the common rises on your right, and the views diminish. The track, muddy in places, is another that follows the boundary between the rough vegetation of the common and green fields, indicative of better soils. After a half mile, or so, the track appears to rise up the hillside towards Woodbury Castle, which appears as just another wood from this lower elevation. However, we know our place and instead of climbing the slope we veer left, into woodland, to meet a sign telling us that we are still on the East Devon Way. On the signpost the direction indicated by the lower arrow is the right one. Ignoring a track to the left continue ahead through the woods on a gently wending path which eventually emerges into less sylvan conditions. 'Woodbury Beacon', believed to be one of, if not the, oldest beacons in the county is ahead to the right high on the hill. It is one of the most distinct landmarks on these low heathland-covered hills and can be seen for miles around, hence its choice as a fire beacon.

Our somewhat muddy track turns away from it to reach a surfaced road. Walk uphill, taking care to stay close to its side as the hill is climbed. At the first gateway on the left is a good view across to Exeter and beyond. On the left a narrow lane rises to join the one we are on and just before reaching the main ridge road over Woodbury Common another road leads off to the left. This is an access road to the Woodbury Park Golf and Country Club. A crash helmet on its sign is something of a giveaway as to its famous owner, former World Champion racing driver and golf enthusiast Nigel Mansell. A short way into this road is a speed reduction sign advocating 10 miles per hour as the maximum speed, not exactly Formula One stuff!

A signpost stands on this junction and points to 'Warkidon's Way' along the 'S' bend, in front of you, towards the golf club. Walk to the end of this 'S', then tail off onto a track leading off to the right.

This track ends at a gateway but about thirty yards before this point the faintest of paths leads

off to the right along the edge of the woodland. Although not an obvious feature, it is the one which will provide the stiffest test of the day, as to stay with it you will need to watch it closely. To your right you will hear the drone of traffic on the ridge road above and soon, ahead on the right, you will see a clump of trees which is where another of the walks starts and finishes in this book, this being the Tumulus car park.

However we will not reach it as our path, of dubious dampness, stays below the ridge to reach a broad, wet, flat area, the sort one would normally avoid. The path, which is really nothing more than a damp water-filled ditch for the most part, crosses the centre of this area. This sort of terrain is like Dartmoor, with the grim sort of conditions underfoot that so many 'enjoy' in a peculiar sort of way. Stay the course along and beside the path, which ends on meeting a clearer, firmer track that climbs a short slope to reach the main road near the Warren, not far from a parish boundary stone for Woodbury. Turn right and head along the raised verge until the entrance to the Warren (Fire Point 13) car park is reached in about 60 yards. Cross the road and go through the car park to pass left of its sign and onto the track leading just to the right side of the clump of trees which lies ahead.

This is a great meeting place of paths and tracks. Head straight over the first tracks encountered and immediately you are confronted with three paths forking in different directions. Take the right

one, which leads downhill into a shallow valley and up the other side, only to repeat the same roller coaster again beyond it. On the second dip the placement of timber beams enables the wet ground to be negotiated with complete dryness, thanks to the handiwork of Fountain Forestry of Spitchwick Manor, this being at Poundsgate on Dartmoor.

The hillside beyond is also wet so more beams help you up it. Ahead of you is Woodbury Castle and surrounding woods. Close to the top of the hill a track leads off left whilst the one we have been following starts to turn toward the Castle. Head off left here to reach the brow of the hill where an extremely broad, rough track is met at a T-junction. Turn left and follow it down the hillside where it soon 'doglegs' to the left.

Today it's a 'common' sight to see troops in their battle dress stalking, walking and crawling about Woodbury Common in all weathers, times of day or night and in all seasons. This has gone on for many years, the great open spaces and tracts of land being ideal for the purpose of manoeuvres or exercises, although some won't see it like that.

Soldiers, in some shape or form, have been part of this landscape since Roman times and some may claim before that, if those Iron Age macho men slung their stones and endured outrageous fortunes in, on and around their ditched and moated hill-forts of this area.

In September 1871 the Yeomanry met at Exmouth to repair to Woodbury Common for their annual drill, whilst in 1873 the assembly comprised the Rifle Volunteers and the Royal Artillery. It was not uncommon for the children of villages like Woodbury to down their slates, forsake their studies and march up to the common to see the fine young men in their uniforms. This was all entered in the school's trusty log book so must have been above board!

Earlier, in the latter part of the eighteenth century and the beginning of the nineteenth, the fear of an invasion by the French brought much activity to the south coast of England. An enormous army camp was set up under the command of General Simcoe. Thousands of spectators massed to watch the various military manoeuvres that the troops were put through.

However, we are out for a quiet walk and this broad track that we are now descending is, in its own way, like a ridge route even though it consistently falls away from the heights of Woodbury Castle. Either side of it are two valleys but this track ignores both to head downhill, above both of them, towards dense woodland. Just when you were beginning to think you might enter the forest another broad track heads off to the right. In the first instance it drops down and then up

a steepish, but short, depression. However, beyond it levels and straightens out to take us back to our vehicle which, if you have had a good sense of direction and keen eyesight, you may have spotted earlier. One small dip is all that has to be encountered just before the car park at Uphams is regained.

5 – From Woodbury Castle to 'Arizona'!

The car park on the south side of Woodbury Castle (Fire Point 15) is the starting point for this stony safari of three to four miles, so make sure that your feet are well protected from the constant contact with the hard-on-the-feet tracks which are found on parts of the route. The 'Castle' is a hill-fort with a moat which runs for almost half a mile, and the road that you have arrived on cuts through this ancient encampment. Originally it wouldn't have been so heavily wooded and the views of the surrounding landscape would have made it an important defensive site. However, the Romans referred to it as Alauna Sylva so there would have been trees. Generations of children have played here, running up and down the moat and ramparts and it has been a perfect spot for 'cowboys and indians' and hide and seek-type games. A cottage is found in the centre of the hill-fort and when I was a child it was a cream tea room. I believe, though I may well be wrong, that a Miss Newton served them. I also recall an outside toilet there, well-populated with big black spiders!

Woodbury Castle has a long history. The first Lord Russell, a Dorset squire, the largest recipient of lands in Devon at the Dissolution, camped here in that fateful year of 1549. His army was made up mostly of Italian and German mercenaries. Exeter was being besieged by Catholic rebels in a conflict which is always referred to as 'The Prayer-Book Rebellion', the Catholics wishing to continue with their church services in Latin rather than English. It was from the heights of Woodbury Castle overlooking the distant city that he rode to relieve it from the Devon and Cornish attackers, mostly farmers and labourers. However, before he did so he had to repel a Catholic attack on his troops at Woodbury Common and then endure another bloody conflict at Clyst St Mary. A lot of blood was spilled in the name of religion and Woodbury Common sadly saw its share.

Between August and November 1980 some scenes were shot on this part of the Common for a cult comedy series called *Big Jim and the Figaro Club*. Most of the episodes were filmed on an Exmouth building site because it was about a group of builders and their strained relationship with their foreman, who was something of a social climber, the men taking every opportunity to take him down a peg or two. It starred Sylvester McCoy, who went on to become 'Dr Who' in a later screen life, the late Gordon Rollings, famous for his Yorkshire Bitter adverts, Norman Rossington and Roland Curram, who was the 'villain'. They had a lot of fun filming on the common, making use of mechanical rabbits, rather than real ones, to achieve the desired footage.

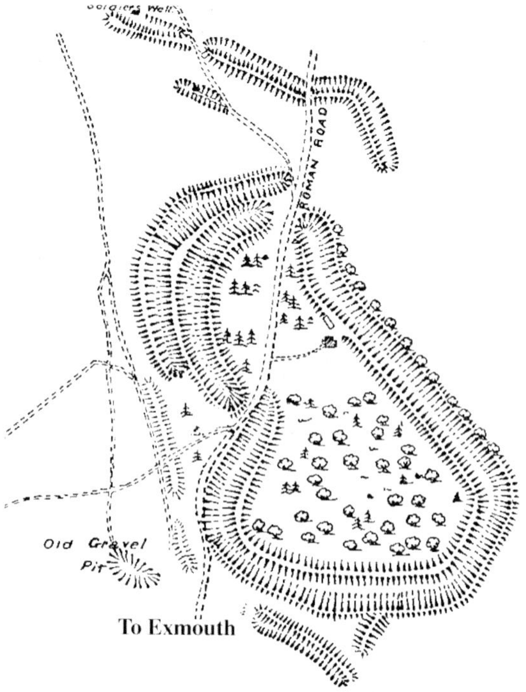

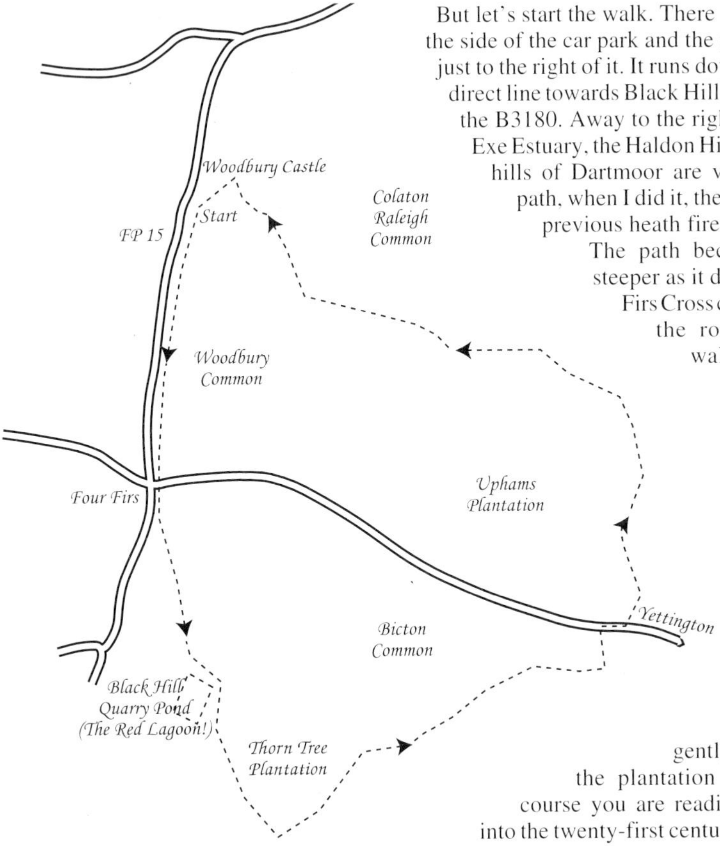

But let's start the walk. There is a small bench at the side of the car park and the path we desire lies just to the right of it. It runs down the hillside in a direct line towards Black Hill Quarry, parallel to the B3180. Away to the right, or the west, the Exe Estuary, the Haldon Hills and many of the hills of Dartmoor are visible. Beside the path, when I did it, there was evidence of previous heath fires.

The path becomes marginally steeper as it drops down to Four Firs Cross car park. Cross over the road carefully and walk across the car park. Where there is another exit back onto the road a track to the left of it leads off on-to the common. This is blocked, like so many, by a padlocked timber pole. There are a few East Devon Way signs, blue arrows pointing our way ahead gently uphill to a gap in the plantation ahead, unless of course you are reading this book well into the twenty-first century, after these trees have reached maturity and been felled! Ignoring other tracks, head through the small wood and just beyond the rise is 'the Red Lagoon', the quarry pond for Black Hill Quarry, an orange blot on the Woodbury landscape.

Cross straight over the junction at the end of the woods and descend the hill towards the pond. This stony path swings around to the left to meet another coming down the hillside on your left.

Keeping the pond, and the orange scars beyond, which someone, with a vivid imagination, said reminded them of Arizona, to your right, ascend the hill in front of you. There are various red and white warning signs telling you to stay out of the quarry.

At the top of the slope the path becomes even broader but still continues to follow the upper rim of the quarry. After several hundred yards of levellish walking, and at the end of this broad long straight, turn left, which is, almost contradictorily, a right angle, to walk downhill along the edge of the plantation on another initially straight track. After a few hundred yards it doglegs left and continues on downhill to reach a dip at the head of another stream which has its swamp to the right of you. Just beyond the dip, at the top of a short rise, is a T-junction with a broad track. Turn right here onto the broadest path.

After about 50 yards is another crossroads and the direction we want is more or less straight ahead but to the left and still the broadest track. After a fairly level few hundred yards the track starts to drop downhill towards woodland where there is evidence, albeit on a small scale, of gully erosion, this caused by heavy rains carving out smaller, lighter materials and washing them down the hillside to leave deep ruts in the track. Fortunately this poses no inconvenience to us, providing we watch our steps down this slope.

The woodlands mark a change of environment and can be extremely wet underfoot. Generally speaking, there is no public way through this wood, or indeed many of the other plantations in the area. However, it is possible to proceed without hindrance. You should encounter no problem provided that you show respect for your immediate surroundings. Therefore, try to stick with the track as it wends its way through this twilight world to reach a small stream, dammed where we cross it to form a small pond. Just beyond the path, for that is what it has become, turns left and an 'East Devon Way' sign points the way up the hillside to a forking of the ways. Head right here and follow this twisting, rising path past young trees. Soon it starts to drop and the road is met near Yettington.

Turn right and take care for this is quite a busy road. The good news is that you are not expected to walk very far along it. After about a hundred yards or so there is a public bridleway signposted off to the left, which is the start of the long haul back up over the common. However, woods first have to be negotiated. At the beginning of this bridleway a gate lies ahead but the bridleway bears right.

When I did this walk for the book there was, at a gateway a little farther on, a sign propped up warning people to be aware of adders. This is where the path enters a coniferous plantation and then bears left uphill. A few hundred yards farther on is another fork and another East Devon Way blue arrow which guides left and onwards through the woods. Continue onwards, with a small ditch on your left, and soon you will notice the open common steeply rising on your right hand side whilst you ascend more gently to reach the top of a rise and a T-junction. Turn left here, shown

once more by a blue arrow, and follow the broad track uphill to the common. Several hundred yards up this track you will see ahead on the brow of the hill a large clump of trees. These are the ones which surround Woodbury Castle. However, to get to it we will have to ascend the long hill using a broad track which appears to us to be left of it. If it's foggy, stay with the track you are on until the edge of the woods and this will bear right and up the hill. Towards the top there is a fork. Take the track to the right, the broader of the two, and soon the edge of the woods near the 'castle' is reached. You will see a low bank close to the edge of this. Pass over it and walk on the straight track which runs parallel to the edge of the trees. At the end of this green and pleasant corridor is a gateway with no gate. Turn left here and follow the ramparts/moat all the way back to your vehicle. You may find that some of the children with you who may appear to have lost all energy are suddenly revitalised and keen to romp around…

By the time you reach your car you may desire an ice cream and there is usually a mobile van at the entrance to the car park on the opposite side of the road. Close by is a fine notice board telling you about the flora and fauna of this heathland area and it's well worth spending a few minutes seeing what the area is all about whilst you enjoy your refreshments.

6 – A Ramble in Raleigh Country

Hayes Barton, the starting point for this walk, was the birthplace, in about 1552, of that famous Elizabethan, Sir Walter Raleigh. His father rented the property from the Duke family of nearby Otterton.

Hayes Barton is built of cob and thatch, in the shape of a letter 'E', and it's believed that this common sixteenth century style was deliberately formed as a tribute to Queen Elizabeth I. Today

it's a private house but it has been opened to the public in the past, many keen historians finding their way to this out-of-the-way spot in the shadow of Woodbury Common. There have been those who have been so taken with the house that they have offered to buy it with the intention of dismantling it in order to rebuild it elsewhere. One wanted to remove it to the USA! If Raleigh could not buy it, and he tried to acquire it in July 1584, from Mr Duke, the owner, then it's sure that nobody else could with such 'traitorous' ideas in mind! For those who want to picture Raleigh's childhood surroundings, this continues to be a cherished location. He arrived in this world in one of the rooms in the west wing with a view onto Hayes Wood and he would have certainly roamed, here so when you walk through it, in a while, you will be in good company.

It was a splendid place to live, in the country and near to the coast where Millais painted his famous work of art 'The Boyhood of Raleigh'. The great Elizabethan soldier, sailor, coloniser, poet and historian had a strong Devonshire accent and was a great thinker, this being borne out by his *History of the World*, penned whilst held prisoner, in a completely different environment to this pleasant place – the Tower of London!

Fortunately for us we are not imprisoned and can enjoy some airy freedom on this lovely circular walk of about three miles. Having parked sensibly near Hayes Barton, walk a short way along Hayes Lane towards East Budleigh and, in the shortest of distances, two footpaths, left and right, are seen. Ours is to the right and runs straight up the hill towards Hayes Wood and Hayeswood Cottage, which is soon passed. One could hardly fail to notice that those who manage this large and attractive wood have gone to great lengths to keep the public to the designated way, vermin traps having been laid in the wood, and so it's a case of following the yellow arrows through it. Dogs must be kept on leads here and walkers should expect a steady climb upwards beyond the cottage.

Higher up the hillside the path is slightly sunken. By following the yellow arrows the 'far' side of the wood is soon reached. Pass beside a large log to reach a distinct lane. This is Hayeswood Lane and we turn right and walk along it, the going good, the gradient gentle, woods to the right, fields to the left, until we reach two circular highway signs. Ignore the track to the left and in about 30 yards you will see a footpath sign at Fire Point 7 leading off to the left, which is the way we want to go. Initially it's through a pleasant avenue of trees but as the path starts to rise it tends to become muddier underfoot. Keep left, as close to the hedge or bank as possible, because after several hundred yards a stile appears on the left, which we cross.

Now you are on a track, muddy in places, where you may have to skirt large puddles. There are fields either side until a gateway is reached several hundred yards farther on. This marks another change of scenery because just beyond we are back on common land once more. On reaching a rough track, at another T-junction, turn right. Below you is a pretty valley with a wonderfully wooded hillside beyond. The stream that runs along this valley is the same one which trickles behind and then beside Budleigh Salterton's main street. Take the next left fork and this will bring you down and around to that wonderful oasis that is Squabmoor Reservoir.

Having heeded all the advice contained on the various signs there, proceed along the right bank of the reservoir taking care not to stub your toe and fly headlong, 'like what I did', on exposed tree roots. The reservoir soon tapers down to nothing and at its top end a timber causeway leads off left across its feeder stream. Ignore it and continue straight ahead. Stay with what appears to be the main footpath, almost orange in colour beneath your feet, and then at this fork, shown in the picture, bear right to reach a car park beneath the trees at Fire Point 5. Go to the exit of the car park and turn right along the road for about 50 yards and you will see a track off on the left. Immediately you are confronted with another choice. Be brave and take the right fork, up the hillside. This next section, which first climbs gently then more steeply, is one of my favourite bits of common and the one featured on the front cover of this book, a picture taken in early September when the vegetation is at its most colourful. As an added bonus, you will not find many other folk

on this moorland, making it ideal for birds. Occasionally a Dartford Warbler may be spied! Others have appreciated the beauties of this area. Walter Scutt wrote this of it in 1936: "What can be more beautiful than the open common with its green and gold and purple-green waves of bracken, gold of furze-blossom, purple of ling and heather; its patches of woodland-dark fir trees, vivid green larch, yellower beech, and tawnier oak; and its clumps of scots-pine with trunks glowing like bars of red-hot metal in the warm light of sunset."

At the top of the hill a track, almost doubling back, comes in from the right. Follow it and, to check you are on the right path, look straight ahead to see the distant triangular-shaped hill/cliff of High Peak to the right and compare what you see with this small picture. The path goes on to soon enter an area of higher undergrowth/overgrowth where a yellow arrow tells us to bear right at the first fork. At the first crossroads of paths head on straight across to walk on the level to reach a surfaced road with a car park on the far side. This is Wheathill (Fire Point 4), a scene in the past of a heathland holocaust when, one March, many years ago, an attempt to manage the vegetation by swaling went out of control. The swalers were working under the instructions of Lord Clinton's head keeper but a keen wind fanned the flames and the Exmouth Fire Brigade were immediately summoned. Despite the

prompt response from the brigade, the fire had spread rapidly, and the area from Squabmoor Cottage towards Woodbury was one great blaze. Such was the heat that telephone pylons were sent crashing down, their wires melted by the intense heat. Cottages in the wake of the spreading fire were gutted and the toll on the wildlife was horrendous, as hundreds of animals and birds perished. In those days the Bystock estate (on the fringe of Exmouth) used these open spaces for their pheasants and the fire couldn't have been at a worse time, for hundreds of nesting birds were destroyed in this conflagration on the common.

Hard though it is to imagine, this area was, during the Second World War, a hive of activity. Here there was a Nissen-hutted town known as Dalditch Camp, referred to many as a 'hell-hole', which housed almost 5,000 Royal Marines. At its peak there were about 378 twelve-man Nissen huts (named after their designer, Colonel P. N. Nissen 1871–1930) and although surviving pictures make them look 'homely' they were anything but! Dank, damp, too cold, too hot, cramped and often insanitary, the troops billeted here found the experience at best 'memorable' but if a more apt description was needed to record their plight, then 'horrendous' would fit the bill. The ground conditions were often appalling and the catering was primitive. Yet many of the thousands who passed through here still come back to visit Dalditch to retrace and revive old memories, ones indelibly ingrained in their minds. Wheathill was the first site to be developed and the complex of buildings later expanded to include 107 huts used for a variety of other purposes. There was even a cinema! Dalditch Camp, nicknamed by some as 'Belsen Grange', occupied much of the area that we cross in the next half mile or so. The Camp was divided into five sections known as Wheathill, Triangle, Hayes, Tuckers and Fryingpans. When the war ended a choice had to be made whether to keep Lympstone or Dalditch. As you walk along I don't really need to tell you which won ... Dalditch Camp closed in 1946.

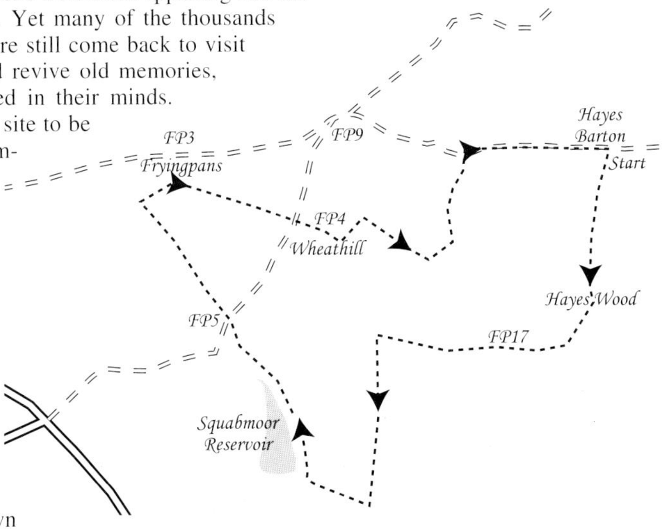

Head through the car park, following its left hand edge, which takes you onto a track. After about 80 yards a large clearing is reached. A narrow path heads off to the left. Follow it and in next to no time it meets another one crossing it. Turn left and descend the hillside through the woods. One tracks leads off to the left a few hundred yards down the slope. Ignore it and continue for another 50 yards or so to a point where our route swings right to follow a more level course across common land once more. At the next fork take the path to the right. Ignoring any side paths, stay with this one until it reaches a very obvious T-junction with a broad path coming down the hillside from the right. Turn left here and walk around the kink of a bend to rise to a broad open space. Cross it to head towards a gateway. As you will see, this is Hayes Wood again and entry into it is neither desired or permitted. However salvation is at hand in the form of the broad track which skirts the wood and our required direction is to the left and generally downhill. Along this section there are one or two places where the track is composed of sand. The track soon brings you down to the road, this being Hayes Lane. Turn right and walk carefully along it back to Raleigh's birthplace and your vehicle.

7 – Venn Ottery Common and a Rugged Rectangular Ramble

Unlike other walks in this book there is no car park, but the lane is wide enough to accommodate your vehicle without too much trouble. The starting point is the most northerly in this book, on Venn Ottery Common. The easiest way to find it is to drive the B3180 road from the Half Way Inn towards Ottery St Mary. About 1½ miles along is a road off to the right at Aylesbeare Hill. Drive along it and in about half a mile take the left fork signposted to Venn Ottery and Tipton.

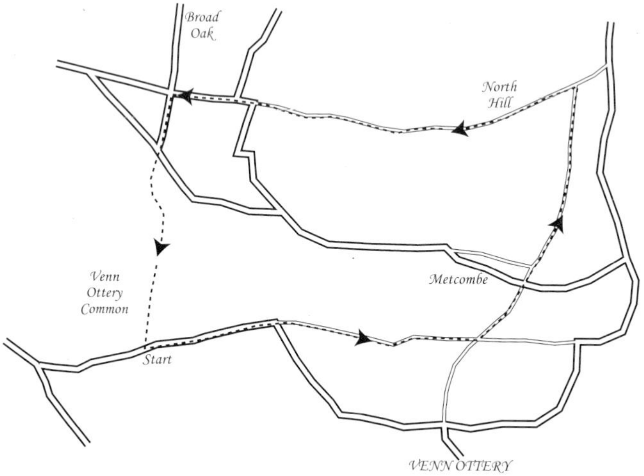

In a short distance this starts to drop down a steep hill where there is space to park. If you park sensibly, close to the start of footpath 33 marked on your left by a narrow gap in the hedge, then you are at the right place. There is some road walking, but not too much, and after rain there are some trench-like puddles which may be hard to avoid. Otherwise this is a healthy stroll of about four miles which should improve your circulation…

Start off by walking down Venn Ottery Hill, towards the wide and beautiful Otter Valley, never a problem for most folks. Stay with the road until it swings right, by a signpost to Venn Ottery. Here you keep your level by walking onto a broad track to your left which carries you onwards and straight ahead. Away to the left Ottery St Mary can be seen, its lovely church of St Mary's visible to those blessed with good eyesight. Also visible are Dumpdon Hill and the flanks of the Blackdown Hills, where Hembury Fort is a notable landmark.

Back over your right shoulder are the commons of Aylesbeare and Harpford, and 'The Lonesome Pine' of a previous walk stands boldly erect on the hill.

Continue along the lane and another lonesome, forlorn, fallen-on-hard-times tree is encountered where a track comes in from the right. A short distance beyond it a track leads off to the left. Take it and enjoy the squelchy, steep drop down to the edge of the hamlet of Metcombe. On meeting civilisation bear left of the first property to immediately reach a surfaced road. Head straight across, passing over a brook, a tributary of the nearby Otter, to head towards a heavily extended and enlarged redbrick bungalow called 'Wild Green'. The track takes you to the right of this and upwards. The route instruction couldn't be simpler because all you have to do is to stick with this lane, for almost half a mile until the next building, on the right side of the lane, is reached. What we might want to forget is that this lane can be very wet and when I did it, after a period of prolonged heavy rain, I got two British Standard Bootfuls of muddy water and a tide mark high up my ankles. Lighter people fare better!

Beyond the detached redbrick building a broad track comes down the hillside from the left. The bad news is, yes, we have to climb it. Fortunately it's not as daunting as it first appears and the top of North Hill is easily achieved. Once more the route is easy to follow. Stay with the track, again muddy in places, for the next mile. Away in the woods to your distant right are the roof-tops of houses at West Hill, one of the more select residential areas of Devon!

Just when you thought that the track was never-ending it bends to reach civilisation once more and evidence of being back in the 'real world' is found in the presence of the Neighbourhood Watch scheme now entered. The track passes the attractive thatched cottage of Higher Fluxton to reach the road.

Soon a signpost is reached. Head straight up the hill in the direction of Broad Oak. Ignore the right turn to West Hill a few yards up the road and walk up the road to the next junction. Although something of a steady slog it should be good for toning your calf muscles! At Broad Oak Cross turn left onto another straight but unsignposted road which, when you reach the far end, you will discover is Higher Broad Oak Road. Along it to the left you will have glimpsed good views of 'Sidmouth Gap'.

At this crossroads continue straight across onto what is also a public footpath as well as an access road to many fine properties. At the next T-junction turn left.

The footpath soon turns to the right to squelchily drop the hillside to cross a stream. Beyond it the ground is wet but by following the yellow arrows higher and drier ground, this being the bottom edge of Venn Ottery Common, is reached. It's quite a climb back up the side of Venn Ottery Hill. We are on footpath 33 and footpath 34 comes in from the left to sociably join us. Head on up the slope to a fork. In the absence of a yellow arrow I chose the left branch and it took me back to my vehicle.

8 – A Hike Around Hawkerland

The starting point for this lovely circular walk of about four to five miles is the car park at Joney's Cross, beside the main Exeter to Sidmouth road about half a mile to the south-east of the Half Way Inn. It sits beneath the 'Lonesome Pine' of an earlier, shorter walk and at almost 500 feet above sea level is quite high by East Devon standards.

At the exit to the car park turn left and walk down the road for a short distance. Almost opposite the lower end of the car park, and on the opposite side of the road, is a log barring vehicles from entering the downhill track that you are about to follow. At the bottom of the slope you will see yet another route marker for the East Devon Way. The pinkish arrow points left along a broad, straight and potentially muddy track which is the way to go. After dropping a little it rises slightly before dropping more obviously. To the right is the country of the Hawkerland depression, an attractive valley where the view is one of woodlands, fields and open commons and, in the right light, it's a picturesque scene.

Just as the enclosed lands to the right begin to impinge on our open landscape, towards the bottom of the hill, a fairly straight track is found leading off to the left. If you are observant you will see there are signposts some 60 yards or so along this path. Walk along it and up to them – you will discover they are on the minor road leading down to Hawkerland.

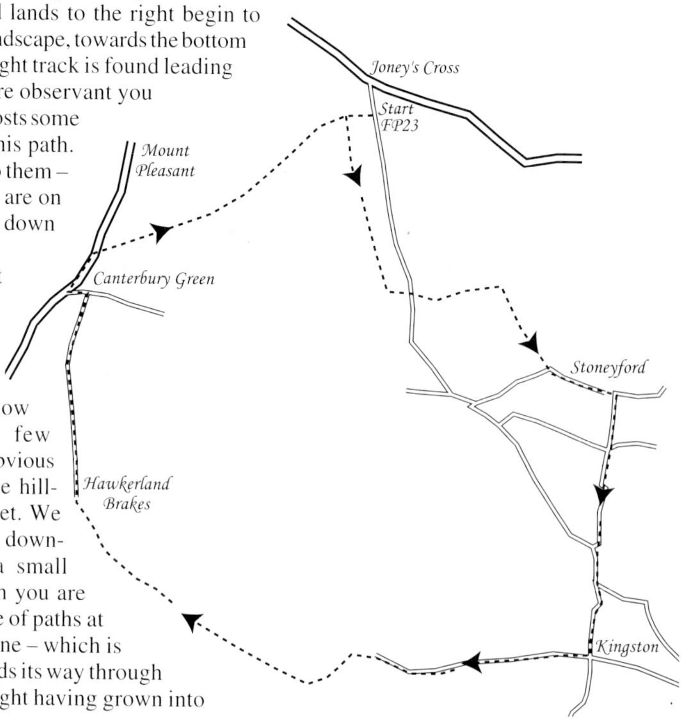

Here head straight across onto the Public Bridleway, preferring the direction offered by the blue arrow in preference to the yellow one this time. In a few hundred yards a more obvious track coming down the hill-side from the left is met. We turn right onto it to go down-hill. After crossing a small footbridge over a ditch you are presented with a choice of paths at a fork. Take the right one – which is the right one! This wends its way through trees, the ditch to the right having grown into a full-blown gully. Once more another broader track, again coming down the hillside from our left, is met and we show ourselves to be creatures of habit so bear right and downhill.

The track becomes more of a rough road where a detached house is met. Continue onwards and downwards to reach a surfaced road at the hamlet of Stoneyford where there are some newer properties.

Head straight on, keeping the stream, which flows on to Newton Poppleford, to your left. After a few hundred yards turn right onto the first obvious rough track, leading up a steep slope. It doesn't cause too much grief and in the short distance of about 150 yards a crossroads is encountered. The lane going across at right angles to us is Naps Lane. Our way lies virtually straight across, with a good view of the open common through the gateway on the angle to our right ahead.

Our path appears to head towards a gateway into a wood but do not be deluded, for it swings sharply left just before it and then sharply right to skirt the edge of this coniferous plantation. The going is pleasant and easy but doesn't last for long, because the track drops down to a surfaced road. Turn left onto it to head downhill. On approaching the bend you will see on your right a fine piece of walling, an excellent example of the use of these large rounded bunter pebbles in such structures.

We are now at Jockeys Hill Cross, the signpost on the junction telling us this gem of information. Head right here towards Stowford, a common name in Devon, the 'stow' often denoting a religious connection in a place name. Almost immediately Kingston Farm is reached, complete with an agricultural aroma. Opposite the conglomeration of buildings parts of the hedge show the deep orange of the local New Red Sandstones, a feature of south and east Devon.

About 50 yards beyond Kingston Farm a crossroads is met. Our way from here is right, up the muddy farm track, an ideal opportunity to show how light on your feet you are when confronted with the sort of primeval oozy mud that only churned-up tracks like this can offer. Farther up I would strongly recommend walking the right side as the preferred option.

There is a point where the muddy track suddenly dries out as the common is approached.

However, it drops into a shallow dip before rising again and this provides a short wet patch of some 30 yards or so, but nothing a hiking hippo couldn't plough through without too much bother.

The lane becomes greener and a public bridleway sign is encountered. Head more or less straight on up the slope, this short bit having been covered on an earlier stroll in the book. About 100 yards on, just around a rising bend which curves left, yet another East Devon Way direction post is encountered. Despite its pointing left, with a neat blue arrow, show that you can be quite contrary and head right uphill onto the open common.

Generally speaking, the higher you climb the better and broader the view. The initial slope is steep but it becomes less so as it ascends the common. If you need a breather, pause and look at the view behind you, one that sums up the reason why so many folk choose to settle here in their dotage. It's a grand landscape! However, should you be unfortunate enough to do this on a misty day, then console yourself that this part of the common resembles Dartmoor. Away to your left,

and beyond the valley, is the grenade-throwing range, but we skirt the danger area to continue ever upwards up the north-eastern side of Colaton Raleigh Common. Eventually, towards the top of the rise, a broad track comes in from the left, from one of the range flag poles, to form a slightly staggered crossways. At this point head straight on over and slightly up again. In about 100 yards another crossways is reached. Once more head straight across it and head downhill towards the woodland of Hawkerland Brakes and the third crossways of tracks in quick succession. Yes, you've guessed it, straight ahead again to leave the open common behind.

This is a pleasant reasonably straight thoroughfare which skirts woodland and farmland to reach a minor road, by a small triangle of grass, after several hundred yards. Here turn left to walk up the road the short distance to Canterbury Green but here we find no Chaucer and no pilgrims, just an attractive farm of the same name offering 'Bed & Breakfast' – but have we walked far enough to merit such pampering?

This next 100 yards is the most dangerous bit of walking in the entire book because, despite being only a B road, it carries plenty of speeding traffic. Turn right along it, stay in single file (even if you are on your own!) to pass the farm, its free-range hens and its churns, to reach a double sign not far away on the right. One is for a public bridleway and the other a public footpath. The latter is the one we want, a stile shows us the one that we require to follow. The path through woods, the southern edge of Mount Pleasant, is not too taxing apart from a few squelchy places and a few scratchy ones, holly bushes lurking with an intent to ruin our natural good looks. Stay with this path, running just above the 400-foot-above-sea-level contour, until it reaches another stile, just beyond a small bridged stream, at the end of woodland some 500 yards or so from the initial stile into it. The desired path up the hillside is the one more or less straight ahead, but the left one of the two choices. Towards the top of it a gap appears between the trees to reveal our 'Lonesome Pine' again, a reminder that we are almost back at our vehicle. We bear slightly right to reach a crossways of tracks that we met earlier. The way is ahead up the hillside to the log blocking off unwanted vehicles. At it we will see the car park opposite, where we parked earlier.

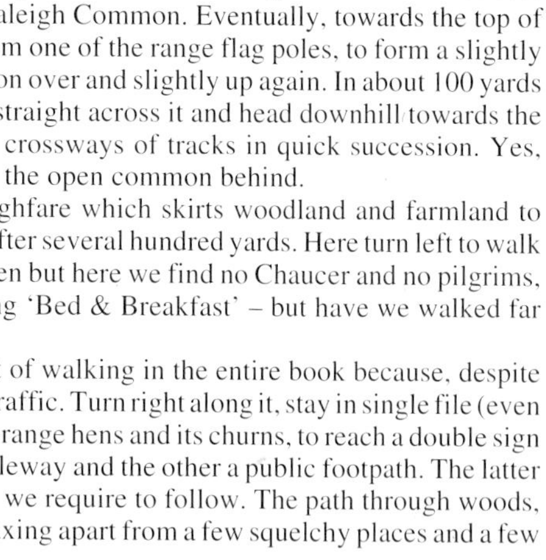

9 – A Circumnavigation of Budleigh Salterton

Between the years 1577 and 1580 Francis Drake completed a circumnavigation of the globe and today, on a much diminished scale, you are going on an epic walk, a circumnavigation of beautiful Budleigh Salterton! Just imagine the wealth and worldliness you will be circling on the longest walk in this book, at about seven miles, and the undoubted 'treasures' that lie within this circle of cottages, colonels and clerics.

There is a Woodbury Common connection, albeit geological, in this walk for it passes the dramatic cut-off point where these East Devon commons meet the sea in abrupt and spectacular fashion.

This is a clockwise walk which begins from the car park at the beach near the mouth of the Otter. Should you wish to 'save a few pennies' in the season it would not be too difficult to find free street parking at nearby Coastguard Road, but not on the sea front itself for this has a time limit of two hours and you don't! Fast walkers could easily bolt around this route in that time but they wouldn't enjoy its subtleties. Out of season, which is undoubtedly the best time to tackle the walk, there is no problem, the Lime Kiln car park being 'free' from the beginning of November to the end of March. In the winter there is no time restriction on parking on the sea front either. I did it on a fine, beautiful February morning and there was nobody about in Budleigh at ten to eight! The car park is named after the lime kilns which were once here. These 'furnaces' processed lime and were often still warm hours after ceasing their task. A tramp is believed to have slept here once too often and to have been 'cremated' by mistake!

On that chilling note walk along the sea front in a south-westwards direction. If you want to avail yourself of the 'highly commended' toilets they are just a short way along on the right.

The beach is a popular one and if you are doing this walk early in the morning you may be treated to the spectacle of some of the town's senior residents appearing at the beach in their dressing gowns. These individuals are not sleep walking but coming down to enjoy an invigorating bathe in the 'warm' waters of the famous Gulf Stream.

I am not sure what it is about 'Salterton' but it has often drawn the attention of comedy programmes who have tended to pull its leg, *The Goodies* and *Monty Python* being just two to have done so.

Stay with the path at the edge of the beach, noticing the wall with ornate shells embedded within it and the bric-a-brac of fishermen's small boats, nets and pots. Enjoy the openness of Salterton as you eventually start to climb, past even more toilets and numerous benches, one of the resort's amazing features for there must be something in the order of a hundred, many with a small plaque remembering people who had a love of this place. They make interesting reading. Kenneth Cant, like so many, "never tired of this view"; Dorothy Atterton is recalled in a two-line verse: "Stay a long time as did she, enjoying Budleigh Salterton by the sea"; whilst Dr J. D. Nelms "... spent many happy hours sailing his little boat in this pleasant bay." Does any other resort as small as this have so many glowing accolades to its beauties?

The benches run out with an increase in the upward gradient but soon more of a level is achieved. For a short while the cliff-top path skirts the edge of 'Jubilee Park', an easy stretch before passing over 'Hackley Quarterdeck', as it is named on my 1906 map, just to be topical. Ignore any side paths and after a slight dip, below a cliff-top knoll, covered in pines, the long climb towards West Down Beacon, which sits atop the Floors, is begun.

The path skirts a small fenced reservoir which lies to the right of the path, and over your right shoulder you will see the fine club house of the East Devon Golf Club. To your left a sign tells you that the cliffs are unstable so stick to the well-trodden track and continue upwards. The golf course is to the right and the vegetation on the right gives way to a wire fence at the 17th tee to provide a good view to the north and east. You may have noticed that on this last part of the climb the pines, the vegetation and the presence of the pebble-bed, bunter pebbles are all reminiscent of the Woodbury Common landscape. This is where the 'Commons' reach the sea.

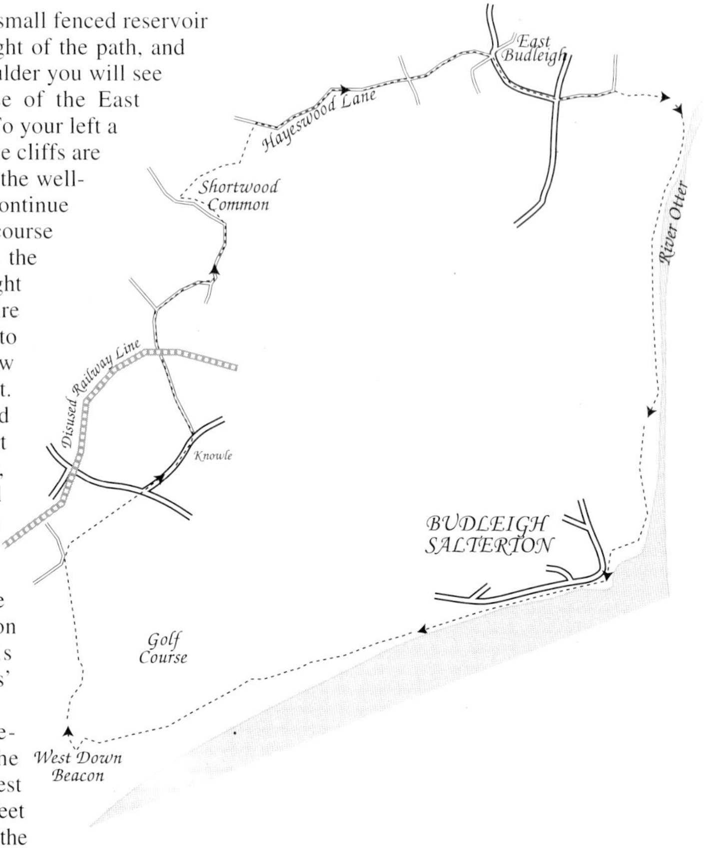

The energy required to reach the bevelled peak of West Down Beacon (425 feet above sea level) atop the Floors is well spent because from the top, on a good day, much of East Devon and can be seen. Dartmoor's range of hills occupies part of the vast horizon and Rippon Tor and Hay Tor, on Eastern Dartmoor, stand just above the distant Haldon Hills. The South Devon coastline is visible, with cliffs beyond Berry Head at Brixham discernible and the resorts of Shaldon, Teignmouth, Dawlish and Dawlish Warren in view. Closer to home the Exe Estuary and Exmouth are clearly spied, whilst the immense Sandy Bay complex dominates the foreground. It is one of the best views in Devon (and there are many great ones). This spot's 'Beacon' name is well justified because in those long-ago times of the Spanish Armada this was one of the sites where a beacon would have been lit if an invasion had been threatened. By choosing prominent spots like this the whole country could be alerted to some potential national danger in a short time.

About 30 yards beyond the Beacon a yellow signpost offers the choice of straight ahead, with Littleham Church directly in view, to Sandy Bay and Exmouth or right, inland, which is the one you will take. The path now wends its way through vegetation of varying heights, sometimes with views of the sprawling growth of Exmouth, Devon's fastest-growing town, they say, almost reaching the Common. Another small reservoir is passed, this being to your left. Much of the flora is of the prickly variety; is this how the term 'scratch golfers' evolved? Joking apart, you will soon see more golfers, just like the hymn book, both 'ancient and modern', enjoying the elevated fairways. The East Devon Golf Club's members were participants in a match against Sidmouth in 1932 with unusual stakes. Each team sent out 16 players, each of whom had to bring a rabbit with them so that the winning team could enjoy a rabbit stew or two! The practice was abandoned to be replaced by a more animal-friendly prize, the winners taking charge of a large painting of

16 rabbits being led, like dogs on a lead, from Sidmouth. The fixture is known as the 'Rabbit Picture Match'.

Turn right at the end of the scrubland to follow the footpath which goes behind the 8th green to veer left to head to a well-defined track. Keeping the same northward direction follow it past the 8th tee, now on your left, into a straight tree-lined lane which drops down to a gate. Pass through it and stop. Do not descend onto the road but first turn right where you will immediately see a footpath, bearing left, that passes between high fences. This path, beyond the human boundaries, becomes a pleasant woodland path for a while before straightening and dropping downhill. On meeting a road at Lilac Cottage simply cross over it and continue through the woods down to the busy road T-junction at Knowle. To your right are the flower beds with the name sign for Budleigh Salterton, greeting those who travel in to the resort; but we are bound straight ahead into Knowle. Cross this busy road with great care and walk along the pavement on the right side of the road into the hamlet ahead. The large white house to the left, standing in its own parkland setting, is Lee Ford. Farther on, beyond the potential watering hole of the Britannia Inn, is Knowle Garage. Opposite, a much quieter road leads off to the left which is our way for just less than half a mile. The small church of St John's, a six or seven feet high wall packed with pebbles, and some attractive thatched cottages are soon passed. The small stream running beside the road on the right is the same one which is dammed for Squabmoor Reservoir upstream and which flows through Salterton downstream. The one feature that is hardest to miss is the towering railway bridge of immense height, no need to duck to pass under this one! On my old map of 1906, it is marked as carrying the 'Exmouth & Salterton Line'.

Just beyond the redbrick railway bridge, which needs repointing, the land rises on our left to the heights of Dalditch Common, one of the smaller commons now, in this area where the commons are all too common!

The road crosses the brook but continues beside it for a while. Just before it re-crosses it a track leads off to the right past Dalditch Apiary, whose name sign bears two beehives but could so easily be mistaken for a bra that Madonna once sported. The reddish track climbs the hill and higher up the expression 'walking beneath the trees' takes on an entirely different meaning. Towards the top another track is met and here you should swing hard left and continue upwards. Just about 80 yards beyond the crown of the hill is an exit to the right, with a footpath sign, offering two choices. Ignore this to walk to the next fork, some 60 yards or so farther on. Bear right here to stroll along the lower slopes of Shortwood Common, a not unpleasant track through wood and scrubland. It curves and then rises to a T-junction and here you should turn right and ascend the hill. After a few hundred yards of good, steady, fairly steep upward stuff the brow of the hill is attained and just beyond it, on the left, is a stile leading into a field. Follow the edge of this field which takes you just to the right of Hayes Wood on the hill now ahead. Quickly you will reach another stile which, when negotiated, sees you in Hayeswood Lane. If you have done the walk earlier in this book, which brought you up it, you will now see what it's like to turn right and go down it!

It is initially steep and sunken but evens out. After rain it can be wet, as water drains off the adjacent fields, but it's good to go downhill and it's a long lane of just less than a mile down to East Budleigh. It's obviously popular with walkers, horse riders and mountain bikers, the trackmarks of each faction etched into the mud.

Ignore the two side tracks, Lillage Lane to the left, soon followed by Little Down Lane on your right, and you will curve your way down the valley to reach the village having 'danced' through the farmyard-influenced road surface.

Just before the junction, notice on the building on your left 'M.R. 1879'. If you are observant you will see other buildings with these initials in and around this area. The letters stand for Mark Rolle, who was a wealthy man responsible for much of what went on in this part of Devon in Victorian times. He laid out the cliff-top golf course, on what was part of his estate, that we passed earlier; he initiated renovation or building work on churches at Beer, Exmouth, Otterton and Budleigh Salterton; built village halls; improved the local water supply and so on. He was High Sheriff of Devon, in 1864, and divided his time by living either in his North Devon home at Stevenstone or at his other stately brick pile of Bicton House, a short distance away from here.

Turn right at the junction opposite Drake's School into what is East Budleigh's Middle Street. Walk along the road, past some interesting signs, and also some more of M R's handiwork, to enter 'Lower Budleigh'. Stay with the main street, accompanied by the still ever-babbling Budleigh Brook, to reach the main road by the aptly-named Rolle Arms, at the equally aptly-named Rolle Cross. Roll on across this busy junction and continue to frogmarch along Frogmore Road, a flint wall on your left being unusual in a land where most walls are 'filled' with large rounded pebbles.

Stay with the lane until Thorn Mill Farm is reached. Opposite is a footpath to the right which will take you past a pumping station and over the trackbed of the Otter Valley railway, the same line that we passed under back at Dalditch. The path is easy to follow on a causeway raised just a little above the level of the Otter's flood plain meadows. It curves gracefully to meet the river at the point where an aqueduct discharges its flow into the Otter.

The Otter is now followed downstream all the way to Salterton. This footpath is well-worn and is about the closest thing to a 'conveyor-belt' that you will find. It is probably the most walked riverside path in Devon but for me it's only interesting when White Bridge is passed and the estuary, now much shorter, shallower and narrower than it was in the past, and its nature reserve are reached. For more details you might like to read another of my books, *Along the Otter*, which reveals all.

Below White Bridge the track continues to skirt the estuary and, if you are interested in natural history, there are platforms where you can watch the comings and goings of the various birds found here. As the end of the walk is reached the view ahead is one of contrast. To the left are the estuary marshes, the 'home ground' for many species, and to the right the verdant pastures of the man-made habitat of the Budleigh Salterton cricketer. The walk, like this book, is now finished. I hope you enjoyed this and all the other safaris, and that now you know the area on and around Woodbury Common that little bit better. In places, off the tracks, paths and bridleways, it is something of an impenetrable jungle of heathland vegetation, but I hope you managed to follow in my footsteps without too many prickly problems.